Bot's Bits

Written by Joanne Reay
Illustrated by Nelle Davis

NORTHWOOD SCHOOL
818 W. LEXINGTON AVE.
HIGH POINT, N.C. 27262

When I'm in bed,
Bot gets up.

Tip-tap-tup.
That's him.

That's Bot!

Two big pans.
Old tin cans.

Lots and lots
of lids and pots.

A cup and a jug.
The dog's red rug.

Dad's big bin.
A safety pin.

Dots of ink,
green and pink.

A bell and a bag.
A big red rag.

Two eggs.
Spider legs.

Cups up top.

Mom's wet mop.

The tip of a bat.
A pan for a hat.

And that's that.
That's Bot.

Then up comes the sun,
and in I run.

Bot's gone!
But I can see Bot's bits.